Midnight Radio

Also by Michael Sariban
At the Institute for Total Recall
A Formula for Glass
Facing the Pacific
Luxuries

Michael Sariban

Midnight Radio

ninety meditations on love and desire

In memory of my wife Joan, who seriously pushed me;
for poet Mark O'Connor, who read my first manuscript;
and for Martin Duwell, most attentive of critics

Midnight Radio: ninety meditations on love and desire
ISBN 978 1 76109 686 0
Copyright © text Michael Sariban 2024
Cover image: Clive Robertson

First published 2024 by
GINNINDERRA PRESS
PO Box 3461 Port Adelaide 5015
www.ginninderrapress.com.au

Contents

After Dark	9
Long Way Home	10
Dead of Night	11
Outlines	12
Victoria Street	13
Loose Change	14
A Bright Morning on Your Balcony	15
Rainbow	16
The Flesh Made Word	17
Adam & Eve Grope for Language	18
Original	20
The Body is like Venice	21
Of Sex and Silence	22
In the Neck	23
The First Time	24
Plain Gold Ring	25
Love Graffiti	26
Emily's Name	28
Cloud Map	29
The Moon Through a Window	30
All About Separation	31
Hang-gliding	32
Black Light	33
The Offer	34
Class Act	35
The Place in Darkness	36
Old House in the Country	37
Geological Time	38
Slipstream	39
Quartet	40

The Trail	41
The Room Upstairs	42
The Cooling	43
Power Play	44
A Parting According to the I Ching	45
The Singer, Not the Song	46
Vampires	47
Another Night, Another Poet	48
Two in the Morning	49
Shortcut	50
Cast-iron Bath With Stars	51
Line in the Sand	53
Driving South	55
Lemons & Limes	57
My First Wife	58
Snowman	59
Lighthouse	60
Transparency	61
Five-finger Exercise	62
Piano	63
Johannes & Clara	64
The Night Shift	65
All in the Mind	66
Photo Negative	68
What Can't Be Held	69
Rock Face With Wattle	70
Half-life	71
Repair Job	72
Inscription	73
On the Eve	74
Jackknifed	75
Bandage	76

A Voyeur Welcomes September	77
Player	78
The Tan	79
Plum-coloured Days	80
The Business	81
Hotel	82
Pleasure & Pain	83
Another Country	84
This Love	85
Saving the Day	86
Saving the Night	87
Crowded	88
Old Flame	89
The Debt	90
The Desire Between Them	91
Whale Song	92
Charcoal	93
Phoney War	94
Little Red Devil	95
Street Theatre	96
Title Fight	97
Truce	99
You Never Saw Yourself	100
All Quiet at the End of the Street	101
Cooling Down	102
Midnight Radio	103
A Night Off For the Moon	104
Acknowledgements	105

After Dark

It's after dark and raining. Every car that
passes just passes the water around, a muffled
hiss that drowns in our ears and revives
and is drowned again.
Rain sprays its trademark graffiti over cars
texting at lights, mixes itself into a soundtrack
that slows or speeds up like heartbeat.
Let's go inside and turn our backs on
the neon signs flashing their gospel above
half-empty towers – advertising reality,
telling us how to connect.

Telling us what to expect. Virtual reality's
so real, it can take buildings out
in broad daylight.
Our own reality's still hardwired just the way
we like it – unaugmented, but enhanced
rediscovering primitive skin.
Let our avatars rehearse their roles,
tonight we won't let them in.

Long Way Home

Outside, the streets are dismal with rain,
cold with early nightfall.
He thinks of the music waiting at home, music
that warms him like Scotch, and some nights
makes up for his life.

Home is a train ride away. The streets, as if
designed for this, convert water into light –
the roadway shimmers, cars shine like trumpets,
their engines muted by rain. Neon signs are
washed clean of their sin.
He's waiting for something to cut through the
talk, through the competing perfumes, through
the beer woven into the carpet.
Out of nowhere a pair of hands sets about
turning smoke-filtered light into sound, which
some will convert into colours.

No trumpets bleating, no sax repeating
some pain he'd rather ignore –
just a piano picking its way through a forest
of snow-laden pines;
just footsteps by the side of a road,
a hitchhiker smudging into the dark to be
neither murdered nor saved.

Dead of Night

When most people have unfolded like cartons
into the flatness of sleep – brains
cocooned in delta waves, bodies rocked
only by breathing –
the night bird appears as if to remind us
of the dense beauty of darkness;
perhaps to seduce us into believing
that the dark is all there is.

Wedged deep in the trough of the night,
we reach for whatever picks us up before
setting us down again.
Some lose themselves in a screen;
some introspect, start confessing things
to the only witness around, though only
the fabulous night bird can be totally
believed.

Ghosts are such a tease:
there you are, hand on hip, acting as if
you still lived here, hearing the night bird
with me – I'd reach out and touch you
or put my hand through you, if only
you would stand still.

Outlines

You're tracing the outline with lipstick
as if there wasn't the slightest chance your
hand could get it wrong –
there's confidence, if you please.
You are giving your mouth its shape, your
arm at the angle I know so well – *this*
is who you'll be for the day, and I'm not part
of the conversation you're holding with
your double.

I follow your hand, the line of your wrist,
an intimacy no less frank than nudity's
full frontal –
and the mirror that watches you so closely
has nothing on my gaze.
At your age, I suppose, you're not as
wary of too much happiness – something
you wear quite lightly most days, like a
compliment, or a new dress.

Victoria Street

There's a string of wasps hanging off a sill,
in love, like me. with old houses –
clinging to their paper tube like kids
to a mother's skirt.
I stand on the landing and ring the bell,
tilting at a windmill of silence, listening out
for clues. The sound goes looking for answers,
but the only answer is sound – it bounces
off the walls like laughter, falls silent
as the phone on the floor.

A door that hasn't opened an inch
is shutting itself in my face. This pilgrim
is on the wrong bus. I turn, catch myself
checking the paintwork like an agent
pricing a sale.
Tomorrow you'll phone, explain it all,
reset my perspective again;
even the wasps know you'll be back,
and are working overtime.

Loose Change

I'm there in your wallet along with some
coins, head resting, it seems, on a deep blue
towel – except I was standing, toes gripping
the sand, facing you, trying not to squint,
naked without my dark glasses.
While you focused on reading the light,
the sea kept breaking it up, taking its reading
of you. Guess you were the first to blink.

Your wallet half open, I stole a quick look –
as if to confirm nothing had changed – and was
almost caught in the act.
I would have been fumbling for words –
unable to play celebrity shoplifter, unwilling
to play guilty schoolboy; and you, I suppose,
embarrassed for me, as something
changed there & then.

A Bright Morning on Your Balcony

and the view, in the absence of water frontage,
not half what it is by night. A sky playing
at innocence, as if sunlight could burn
the world clean.
Struck by the light, the tea in our cups
is the colour of dark lipstick, glows like one
of your bowls.
The necklace is back in its drawer; you're
not much into adornment, can wear silence
like a dress. You push your cup aside.

I watch your mouth, hesitate; you are
looking at something behind me. Whatever
is in the air, it will resist us for now.
You spread your hands on the table, as if
asked to show you're not armed – an irresistible
frame, had someone been filming.
No one was, that morning years ago, when
something had seemed within reach,
then moved on like a tram.

Rainbow

The dam squats its vast flatness
between us and a line of hills – Loch Ness
with no hint of a monster.
Eastertime, families, picnics – the patent
rightness of it all, the comfort of congregation.
Some older children flip their canoe, right it
somehow, clamber in, immortal inside
their life vests.
My new companion points with her fork
to a rainbow arcing over the lake, as if it had
chosen this modest assembly for some
clear angelic message –

its playschool pastels look impossibly frail,
as if a gust of wind might dissolve them,
or a kite slice them in half.
For now, she tolerates my mood, having
heard my side of the story; I don't try to probe
her belief. And the rainbow? – not quite
consolation, some kind of light relief.

The Flesh Made Word

A species that sheds tears. A species
that embellishes, wears totems on the skin,
love beads around the ankle – culture
as life's gift to life.
An energy guiding the hand: a piece
of charcoal, a knife.

Infants squeeze out of the womb, bodies
appearing naked to some in the absence of
ornamentation – a *tabula rasa* billboard,
skin may determine their station.
The briefest inscription on bare flesh
advertises a story, makes the most personal
sense; skin issues an invitation, or serves
as electric fence.
Hearts migrating from sleeve to skin
may prove the most unkind – someone's
love proclaimed as fact, long after
they've changed their mind.

Fuelled by a passionate eye, skin
is happy to illustrate how flesh can be
reborn as word –
a mind intent on seeing itself, skin
dying to be heard.

Adam & Eve Grope for Language

1

Up to their necks in self-indulgence, this pair
set loose in the Garden –
the original clay animation, in hyper-real 3D:
warm rain, and a fragrance to die for.
Nothing they'd ever want to change
this oh-so-benevolent sky for.

Her special fascination:
a peculiar plant that waxes & wanes,
its reddish-brown foliage ticklish and soft
to her curious mouth and hands;
a plant that exudes such pungent sap
before drawing back into itself – amazing
what you can think without thinking,
catching your breath in the grass.

Paradise rolling out all around them,
one step ahead of their feet: clear water,
fruit-laden trees, the wildlife well-disposed.
There seems no need to name a thing,
not even the fact of each other.
Eve content with her one hot date,
not dying to be a mother.

2

The day they bit into the apple,
caught in the act on Security footage,
the game was clearly up.
Irradiated with knowledge, they found words
tumbling round in their heads. Started
arguing, even in bed.
She took to teasing her companion about
his wilful banana; and found herself defined
in turn as his favourite papaya –
new-found metaphors clearly not pleasing
to a disgruntled God.

The sword of irony proved no match
for the flaming metal of angels –
in no time at all they were sent packing,
too busy for ages to think, too tired
to be talking dirty, what with the kids & all.
Wondering if it had all been a dream,
the good times before the Fall –
two minor gods in reality mode, stuck
on a challenging set; making their lines up
scene by scene, washing their mouths
out with sweat.

Original

For busy hands, too, the devil
makes work. Can't believe the things
we permit each other, having dispensed
with the rules; settling for improvised
heaven, leaving hellfire to fools.
Wrapped in creature comforts – our original
fur and skin – we are determined to
replicate all of original sin.
Since there's nothing left to invent,
we're free to be unoriginal, trusting
each other's intent.

Still, it's hard to silence the brain.
Idly we ponder the meaning, the original
purpose of sin; noting the changes of
fashion, the sins that are out, or in.
And we don't give a damn who's judging,
or if angels can dance on a pin.

The Body is like Venice

The body is like Venice – it's all
been said. Regardless, we can hardly wait
to hear it all again. Touch me right now
and I will spout grace & salvation, speak
in tongues, or lapse happily into cliché –
then wait for the body to stop the mouth
with its own version of truth, a trick
not confined to the young.

The body has always been more than willing
to take up where speech leaves off, skin's
never lost for words; bliss never tries to seal
our lips, preferring to prise them apart,
while body and mind argue the toss about
who has first claim on the heart.

Of Sex and Silence

Orchids in a midnight garden succumb to a
ripening daytime lust under the eye of the moon –
seduction right under our noses, vibrations
we cannot detect, sounds only flowers
can hear.
Colour and scent in collusion, all languid folding
and unfolding, tongues flowering in the dark – sex
in wild profusion, orgasms spilled noiselessly
into the humid air, only the buzz and hum
of insects advertising each climax.

Orchids, we're told, are the very sap
and tang of the erotic – fabulous exotic lives,
but with nothing to say for themselves.
It seems to me that you and I share
the better of good worlds, don't need
to be so discreet.
You put your mouth to my ear: the crudity
of language, the flowering of sound.
Words good enough to eat.

In the Neck

i.m. Dorothy Porter

Old Transylvania, timeless haven for legions
of the undead – folklore and schlocky horror
intertwined as deliciously as our fingers
in the back row.
Midnight, French windows, lace curtains blowing,
a lightly clad beauty asleep – some hoping for
a miracle, some of us hot for the vampire –
long ago, when evil was pure black & white,
and blood trickled dark as ink; when sex
and fear held hands, content to leave it
at that.

Remote now as celluloid, to remember
kissing her neck – all first-love clumsiness,
all sudden pink confusion, masked
by the helpful dark.
First love? Now there's a vampire
to leave a window open for, happy to be
sprung. Discerning bat, swooping only
through the casements of the young.

The First Time

Close enough to see eye to eye, they
agree there will be no soundtrack; a television
looks down from the wall with a grey
unblinking eye.
The fireplace that happened to come with the
place is mixing drama with shadows –
flames that come with a history, before
persona or style.
Shadow enough to undress by – the quick
surprise of each other like the smell of
warm rain on asphalt.

The landscape of the young – it's an ache
to recall it, a tease.
Players may feel they have fewer, or more,
dice to play with each year; still, everyone brings
an ego, and some untranslatable fear.
Everyone works out quickly enough what
the other person wants; what they might get
in return is never instantly clear.

Plain Gold Ring

The young couple next to me take it all in
so earnestly, regardless of the poem.
The wife has an interesting face, and is
Halloween-pumpkin pregnant.
Her hands are strong, a year-round tan
sets off their thin blue veins; her brown feet
are at one with their sandals.
Her wedding ring is plain, as is a large gold
earring, the old fortune-teller kind.
They seem secure in themselves, in
each other, exude equal and opposite calm;
look composed, as if for a sitting.

His look is part patience, part resignation –
in profile it's hard to be sure.
Her face – she has briefly turned her head –
is Swedish farmer, or Ukrainian folk tale, or
a girl you talked to in Wales; in any case,
motherhood in the making, waxing like
the moon.
Looks like the baby is soon – home birth,
I'd be willing to bet. His breath smells of
raw onion; the baby will be fine.

Love Graffiti

1

We long for someone to stencil *True Love*
across our expectant hearts –
our graffiti-resistant hearts, that crave more
than aerosol spray; our optimistic hearts, beating
under T-shirts that claim to love New York
to bits.
The text, of course, being optional –
it's the trademark arrow through the heart
that lights up your life like a stadium.
Wet concrete captures the flightiest heart,
but may not hold it for long; walls offer
no guarantee.

Trees, like emails, continue to spill
secrets we'd forgotten – we spot an incision
left unfinished, as if stopped in its tracks by
a ranger, or a burst of indecision;
we decipher some weathered initials, and
oddly, they match our own.
First love – nothing else feels the same?
To some it's a monochrome movie, perhaps
just a single frame.

2

In front of cave paintings we hold our breath –
to see breath like ours congealed on a wall,
to realise that saliva like ours was worked
into the pigments – and tend to retreat
into silence.
As the past shuts its door in our face, the
prickling at the back of the neck – we'd kept it
to ourselves – slips into a past of its own.
Returned to the world, we say something like
awesome, having recognised ourselves;
we may feel disarmed, unimpressively recent,
with nothing left to add. Or experience
a weird kind of love.

3

Sometimes a heart, etched in wet concrete,
stops you in your tracks: a wide-open heart,
so much larger than life, to hold – spread
your arms – *this* much feeling.
You'll probably scan the inscription –
initials, or a pair of first names either side
of a verb, or an arrow –
a sequence of data decoding the genome
of adolescent love. Details of which had
seemed, till that moment, lost in a fold
of the past.

Emily's Name

Emily lives above the tideline, renting
the sand for a day or two just below the
bike path.
A name not scratched just any old how –
identity encoded here, and more than a trace
of longing – a style that's been practised,
got right.
An advertisement for the self, more
ephemeral than billboards – the calligraphy
being the message, intended, perhaps,
for just one; an hourglass *Eternity* that
will endure till skateboards or bikes
erase it.

She'll be cold tonight, but sleeping in style –
the tail of the 'y' curling under her as the
belt-buckle *'E'* reins her in – most likely the
work of her own hand, but I guess that's
an innocent sin.
Her body temperature will plunge, but
the passion that inscribed her name will
glow under a know-it-all moon, warm
and steady as heartbeat.

Cloud Map

Children know more about shapes than
we do, know the object precedes the word.
At home with the surreal, they see whole
menageries in clouds, reproach us
if we can't.
Some adults, in secret, persist in this folly –
like this morning, stopped at lights, finding myself
discerning Australia in an ocean of woolly cloud,
inverting Google Earth.
Could have marked my town with a coloured pin,
and felt, for a moment, like a homesick expat
scanning another ice-floe sky for the first
smidgen of blue.

I kept peering into my monochrome map as if
trying to pinpoint my childhood –
zooming in on my street, on the houses,
the face of a girl at her window, now just as
unlikely to find me. Had to blink her away,
as cars started honking behind me.

The Moon Through a Window

You'd slip out of their fancy house, past
the sleeping fiancée, past a bulldog
too old to hear.
A phantom taxi would drop you off, you'd
tap on the window and I'd help you climb in,
while in the next room my mother slept on,
patiently crossing the long dark bridge
between two cigarettes.
Guilt never got a look in. You'd be the one
facing the moon, your eyes jet-black, skin
half-Chinese, slippery as mine.

Tonight's moon is flooding a window
in a room we'd not recognise – returning
on cue, like a burnt-out detective to a
case that won't leave him alone.
I remember your skin, if I think of you,
your face cool in the sharp morning air
as we stop to flag down a cab.

All About Separation

Clinging tightly to a raft on an anonymous ocean –
just another water dream, to be filed behind
dreams of flying.
The raft, this time, morphs into a woman –
almost submerged, I am towed to shore holding
on to her waist-length hair.
I am safe on a beach, but she's vanished.
Must all dreams be about separation?

Last night, in someone else's house,
I dreamt of an unknown woman, tugging at me
from her side of the bed like I was a stone
to be turned;
dreamt of a tongue beginning to map me
but stopping before it was done.

I woke, like before, as if washed up on sand,
moonlight and the sound of surf intruding
through half-open blinds;
someone's absence all over my skin,
fine as the dust on the slats.

Hang-gliding

The thermals here can save your life
or drop it like an egg; steer you away from
powerlines, or funnel you into a tree,
lucky to break a leg –
an Icarus with melt-proof wings, though
not above a fall. The view's supposed to be
worth it; the thrill is something else.

That year, strung out on too many options,
I was wondering if perhaps Russian roulette
had come bundled up with my genes;
and how it might feel to stand on the brink,
swallowing a last mouthful of fear, plunging
into a current of air – all nylon wings
in bright racing colours – my life
a rose-stem between my teeth, arms
spread to catch applause.

It would have been just to impress you –
your, needless to say, interesting face, those
eyes, your sweet & sour breath.
All that just to get inside you, nine lives
for a little death.

Black Light

Our words have stubbed themselves out
like butts, leaving the ash of sense.
You will get out of bed without a word,
predictably enigmatic, and make your way
down the hallway –
determined steps, as if you intended
walking naked out the back door.
But you'll stop in the kitchen and pour
a drink, resisting for now the cigarettes
you are giving up one by one.

I'll find myself listening, a reluctant spy,
for a break in your resolve; wondering if that
willpower might one day extend to me.
You'll appear in the doorway, glass in hand,
observing me, still silent – standing not
so much in shadow as under a cowl
of black light.

The Offer

The party had run out of conversation
and the songs were repeating themselves.
We'd just met, clicked over musical taste,
and were picking up what was left of our wine
when I offered to drive you to your place –
only half-taken with you, my mind on
the stand-off back home.

You showed me your room and
the mark on the wall where your boyfriend
had thrown a knife at you, jealousy's
body language –
you'd understood, even as you ducked,
he was only trying to scare you.
To prove that you weren't in the least –
my signals misread, or not – you showed me
your breasts but soon understood they'd
best be covered again.

It would have been smart to leave sooner,
backed out, with my girlfriend for cover;
it's OK you wrote on a scrap of paper,
but I bet it's *him* you forgave.

Class Act

He'll forget about the flowers on cue,
the harbour-front restaurants, his credit card
bruised and bleeding.
He'll forgo the best seats in the theatre
and at interval her smug friends, ex-lovers
everywhere.
He'll learn not to notice fabulous clothes,
to tune out an upmarket accent – vowels pitched
in the clean tones of money even while talking
dirty; sex on tap while he was the flavour,
messages clogging his phone.
The Audi back to her place, a taxi to
take him home.

He'll go back to missing the good old days –
the odd red rose when he remembered,
her place on Friday nights.
French fries and beer, the half-watched
movies, her face all smudged but there in
the morning in the shower that always
ran out.

The Place in Darkness

What is it he's after – something he lent you,
that tie left behind in your wardrobe?
Does he think you'll change your mind?
What is it he's after with night coming on
and no lights in the house, bruising his
knuckles on your door, and you not
about to answer.
He'll get sick of it, wait and see.
I note your untroubled dismissal, glad
I'm not bruising mine.

You settle yourself back on me.
Hard, under the warmth of your skin, to
imagine myself out in the cold, standing
on the other side of a door with only
my anger to hold.

Old House in the Country

We got ready for bed
on what could have been a
less than welcoming floor;
you made the crickets in that room
sound like a love song
sung backwards

it was still quite cold and our
hosts asleep when you sliced me an
orange and I poured some milk as
a spider exploded like a dark star
from its extravagant web

and we watched small birds
skim like a rumour over paddocks
awash with dew.

Geological Time

Your friends still live on the block they chose
when they chose to leave the city.
Year after year the roads have stayed put
in their hard beds of clay and gravel; the car
seems to know the way.
The trip never fails to mess with your mind –
you feel if you turned your head she'd be there,
but resist reaching across.

On days of such focused longing, you see
the land as if for the first time – like you
may not see it again –
the granite-strewn paddocks, the sheep
glued to slopes, old stumps blackened by fire –
an installation as random and fixed as
the years now layered like coal.

Slipstream

What's changed? A fair bit – new partner,
kids not an issue now. Another not-so-new car.
But the stereo's great, glowing cool green
in the galaxy of the dashboard.
The song playing now is so achingly good
digital couldn't improve it. It's AM to the core –
same hook, same resolution. Same flash
to the day we first heard it –

the radio faithfully channels the sound
as if it knew us back then. What's changed,
except the skin we remember, except you are
thirty years out of reach in the deep space
of analogue time. Lost in the slipstream
you'll never catch up, and anyway,
would you still want to.

Quartet

We sat around a table drinking, you and I
still very new. Your friends were reading from
a collection of Latin American poets –
the language of holy seduction, each translation
a broken mirror.
One of the voices was soft, picking its way
through the English words as if through a minefield,
or flowers – though it belonged to a violent man
whose fate would soon read like statistics.
The gentler man, who knew Arabic,
was drawing the harsh Spanish consonants
through the needle of his throat.

The politics of the moment hung in the air
like the smoke we breathed freely back then.
We drove your friends to their new apartment,
walls still as bare as the floor – drank more
wine by candlelight, played music too loud.
The four of us made a marvellous pair,
but two would end up a crowd.

The Trail

She's back on the mainland, he doesn't
know where. Three days from her door-slam
he feels free to emerge out of tranquillised
tragedy – his 'Venice fever', he calls it,
happy to steal the phrase.
Aware of his folly he'll retrace their steps,
half-believing someone he meets may have
something to tell him; no hope of finding
a trace of the perfume quickly erased
by diesel.

He'll stop at a church they'd once been in –
now secretive and dark – as if damp stone could
retain her presence like that of a certified saint.
God, he couldn't live here – the water,
its ruthless patience, the smell of wet rope,
the rats.
He's irritated again – the revolving-door tourists
who don't speak the language, the pigeons,
small children, the cats. The paintings
that nailed the place long ago, and don't
say a word about now.

Tomorrow he'll end his pretence of salvage,
check messages, book a flight. Arrange lunch
with an ex in Rome.
It may be some time before he returns,
following fresh scents on the street like a
cat relearning a house.

The Room Upstairs

One winter unstitches their marriage at last,
little that needs to be said.
Who knows why *that* particular winter –
as random, he guesses, and as determined,
as a button coming loose.

Could have been any year, any season, all
of the children long since vanished, swallowed
up by their lives.
As he himself has been disappearing
into the irresistible promise of yet another
obsession.
She's been taking it out on the firewood,
kindling flying like skittles. Meals have
the flavour of mime.

She's spending more time upstairs, which
has always been safe from floods, though the
silence keeps rising like damp.
When young and still attending church
she was terribly nervous of voodoo, but is
now doing things with pins.
Keeps watering plants that don't need it,
contemplating new sins.

The Cooling

The last of autumn accelerates like a spool
of film rewinding, and we are unravelling with it,
cooling before our time.
The rain hangs about, no longer pleasant;
soon cold nights may try to sabotage
our arm's-length cohabitation.

Driving home from an evening with friends
we dip up & down a roller-coaster – wet bitumen
shiny as whales – past acres of headstones
where children once played till nightfall
would send them packing.
Sweeping past the tree-lined allotments
of the incomprehensible dead, we wonder
how long they'll retain their grip on this
premium real estate

We too should be wary now –
we've marked a day on the calendar, precise
as a date cut in stone, irrefutable as winter:
we will learn to live alone.
Seems our best prospect now, after years
of flailing around – far better to lie in
separate beds than deceive ourselves with
the counterfeit truce that can sneak up
under the sheets.

Power Play

Took ages to find a site, daylight not
waiting for them. The tent little more than a
flimsy membrane meeting winter on winter's
terms; some kind of neutral ground.

Zipped into a nylon cocoon they confront
each other anew, novelty almost making up
for the stones under the ground sheet.
In due course they'll emerge into floodlit night
to piss under the nose of the moon, frost
whitewashing the grass –
naked in their camping bravado, bodies
pale as blanched almonds.

By morning she might well have made up
her mind, it's serious at her age.
Just before breakfast she captures him,
one of a pair in a juggling act, head poking out
of the tent – snap-frozen in her snapshot,
a smile shiny as chrome: disbelief,
if only she knew it, foreign once more
in her clothes.

A Parting According to the *I Ching*

You were my eyes on the walking track
up to the top of the range – the drop somewhere
off to the right, cold air clinging to our legs.
A full moon kept losing itself in cloud –
we'd left it hanging over the valley in its white
rice paper shade, continued while the rest of the
party kept stopping to take in the view.
Even with the moon obscured, the dark glowed
like obsidian; night was feeding us sounds
through its headphones, an owl was
patrolling its space.

We'd stopped noticing the cold. You talked, with
your normal intensity, about *The Book of Changes* –
open, back home, on your desk – how
it had helped you discern a direction, clarified
your thoughts. Clinging to rationality, I was
resisting its instruction though change, like
some huge inflatable bird, was flapping
its wings all around us.

Damp leaves were muffling our steps.
The moon had turned into a tarnished coin, stars
couldn't make up the shortfall; I could no longer tell
if you were ahead or had chosen to fall behind.
Time was on some kind of hold.
My feet seemed to lose touch with the ground;
I could hear your voice, distant now, still advocating
change – an ending is nothing if not change –
but the Earth now looked improbably small,
and I couldn't see a way back.

The Singer, Not the Song

She sings with that Latino catch in her
throat – a cookie-cutter voice designed to fit
the shape of your passion – in the flesh,
if you can believe it.
You're hooked on the charge in her voice,
your skin registers voltage –
she's a finely honed machine for sparking
genuine lust, fictitious longing, and/or
a deep discontent.

In the car park a cold shower of stars
is nowhere near cold enough.
You are taking her home between
your ears, your tail half between your legs;
in your bag, a thin slice of her life –
a flake, Cohen might have said.

You'll sink to the floor, content to go down
with a film of Scotch on your tongue –
transfixed, caught like a hapless rabbit
in the crossfire of your speakers. Not
quite in the flesh now, but close.

Vampires

We've shaken hands, exchanged addresses,
gone home with each other's book –
I expect you'll savour the taste of my blood,
you know I'm wild about yours.
The old addictive rush will again come
shooting up our veins; we'll scour every line,
see where we connect, then stare down
each other's ambition –
we'll be enemies, neighbours around a well,
jockeying for position.

If they must, let our poems face off at sunrise
for a proxy fight to the death; while we
sleep in our customary beds, breath
to familiar breath.
The smiles on our lips will give nothing away
to partners too discreet to enquire why
our necks are freshly bruised.

Another Night, Another Poet

If I were to show you another poet, claws
sharp as that nightmare on Elm Street, would
you thank me or start resenting the fact
I'd caused you to furrow your brow –
as if you'd walked in on a fully clothed man
soaking in your bathtub?
Who wants to bleed unwanted thoughts
onto a freshly-scrubbed floor; who wouldn't
rather quickly return to the way things
were before?

This poet you've just handed back –
will you pretend he's a paper tiger, or admit
to hearing screams?
OK, you're right, I suppose it's time
we were getting ready for bed. Let's agree
things are more or less as they appear,
while nightmares not of our choosing
spike the graphs of our dreams.

Two in the Morning

It's two in the morning, the fireplace
near enough to dead.
Cold air is working its way through my clothes –
the price for that wide-screen glass, the view
we deduct from the rent.
There'll be frost on the lawn in the morning,
ice to nudge off the windscreen –
winter, too, has a one-track mind, determined
to make its point.
Down the hall, someone who'd been waiting
to warm me has succumbed to regular breathing,
to a more dependable lover.

I can see myself gingerly lifting the bedclothes
the way a bear might tug at a tent flap,
imagine the cold log of my body easing itself
into warmth –
more than enough to make me horny, but
my midwife hands won't let go of the poem
struggling to emerge.

Shortcut

Out of essentials, out in the drizzle
of early autumn rain; doing our best with
one raincoat, body-to-body warm.
Our first night together behind us, the
future too wide to measure.

A shortcut you've found, though you too
don't belong in this riverside suburb you're
renting, its high walls, neurotic dogs.
We're taking the hilly streets in our stride,
walking like the young; if we stopped, would
we recognise each other –
hair plastered to our faces, clothes slowly
getting wet; the solidarity of bare feet
signalling new beginnings.

The ground is soft, almost soggy now,
but pitted with sharp-edged stones that are
starting to give me grief;
I try to ignore them, think of our shoes
back home under your bed.
Now you're striding ahead, a few steps
in front – as close, and as distant, I suddenly
feel, as you may ever be.

Cast-iron Bath With Stars

That year we were renting a workers' cottage
besieged by parking meters, yet almost
untouched for a century –
a fireplace with bricks stripped back to the kiln,
and a cast-iron bath on the back veranda, perched
on Victorian claws.
Only a mile from the GPO, it had resisted
renovation, had sat out both World Wars, aligned
east-west to the end.

Leaning back, soaking up its history, we'd
watch the first tentative stars through gaps in
the rough metal roof.
Away from the draught the baby made do
with a tub on the living room floor – safe, but
warmed by the fire. No one was looking
for more.

History is a radio station waiting to be
tuned in to. We were hooked on timber & stone,
history's flesh & bone – a dwelling configured
just so, spaces more vividly alive for being
not of the present;
a structure that had smoothed out the past
and might yet do the same for us –
a small marvel, a survivor, an affection
we could readily name.

An affection that couldn't save us, though
it dogged our divergent steps for years,
roaming our heads at will.
A past that had kept trying to catch us,
but couldn't make us stand still.

Line in the Sand

Tea-tree and paperbark, first signs of the
longed-for transition – scrub converting to beach,
light changing its religion.
Children would peer out of back-seat windows
for a glimpse of white between trees –
dazzled by an alchemy that turns everyday earth
into sand; face to face, at last, with the ocean
and what it might dare them to do.

We'd first dipped our toes in sand and water
on opposite sides of the world, but had ended up
equally hooked, the beach never failing to
lash us back to childhood.
We'd gravitate to fibro motels built mainly
for calm weather, whose neon signs often as not
worked better than the showers –
their small bare rooms would hold us close
while we dreamt of more of the same.

*

We could draw a line in the sand and say
it was *this*, it was *here*, that we foundered, and
date it precisely as shipwrecks. But sand is
too shifty for that, changing its constitution,
like us at the mercy of tides.
On a rainbow beach, who can unpick
algae from layers of sand – bands of colour
secure in their beds, though chaos rules
at the edges.

Fuzzy logic couldn't save us from ourselves,
our fear of uncertainty. Beach sand and
dreams disappeared down a plughole, ocean
reverted to ocean.
Poised on the brink of nightmare farce,
we disengaged so thoroughly neither comedy
nor grains of sand could put us together
again.

Driving South

Driving south, dunes on his left, the highway
hugging the coastline; sensing the ocean's great
black engine behind the sound of the road.
He winds down the window, is hit by the cold;
stars, instantly magnified, seem about to pour into
the car – small hailstones, pulled up mid-flight.
His face is soon numb, a small price.

Friday, and speeding towards the weekend,
and also towards the next parting – Sunday night's
mantra of drawn-out goodbyes date-stamping
their time together.
A large steel shed, not quite to themselves –
the far corner her mother's space. She's taking
care of the place, happy away from town.
Blankets, they hope, will help muffle the sex,
at least one of them feeling at ease.

He'll get up to piss, a truckload of stars
spilling like unsecured cargo, the dunny a lone
white sentry box halfway up the rise –
or he'll stand in the moon's uncritical spotlight,
all the snakes beyond the shadows snap-frozen
in winter sleep; hurrying back to a body that's
now breathing too deeply to notice.
Smoke in the air at breakfast time, birds
hanging out for scraps. Come Sunday night
her mother will stand there as if needing to
watch them hug.

Driving north, taking the inland road, the sea
well beyond his hearing; climbs and descents
as familiar now as a much listened-to tape –
say *Under the Milky Way*, which opens up
the whole sky.
The windows are closed, locking in a scent
that will play with him for days. A fortnight before
she returns – a roadblock without a detour;
driving away from, driving towards her, while
a copper moon rises like bread.

Lemons & Limes

You'd always have lemons around the house,
in bowls, if the weather allowed – still life
released from its canvas.
Or you'd invade the fridge with a bagful,
pushing the crisper's envelope, displacing
my hoard of apples, or the last refuge
of grapes – a heap, a cluster,
a hive of lemons swarming in the chilly air,
irreducible yellow. Your pleasure never
turned sour.

Lemons & limes were your badge, signalling
presence much like a perfume;
all the same I never cared much for limes,
smug in their acid green skins.
Your salad dressings were something else,
standard alchemy to you. I save time
by not trying to match them.
I live without lemons, perhaps to prove
I can live alone, without talismans, without
your astringent smile.

My First Wife

My first wife, younger even than me,
first taught me how to dance – the basic
but essential skill of shifting the weight around,
succeeding where high school had failed.
We'd move it at parties, dancing with strangers
if we'd had some little tiff;
we were off & running, trying to keep
in step with the spiralling sixties. Juggling
ideal and reality, some were falling
on their face.

We crashed too, in our own good time.
But children – that was hardly a stumble,
we fell in with the grand design.
So much else we owed each other then;
in the end, we wrote off the debt.
My first wife taught me how to dance,
it's something you don't forget.

Snowman

Late January in a city we're visiting for a
week. Small mounds of snow on doorsteps,
like bulky welcome mats.
Not our element any more, not since our
distant childhoods – undocumented winters
that are personal folklore now.
Hesitant in the face of this stuff we feel
too grownup to throw, we're like Mr & Mrs
Snowman, targets for little children who can
tell aggression from games. Like any good
animation, our lips are moving in sync.

Guess we're happy enough, these days.
Content to take what we can from this place,
and its polished indifference; its crisp,
imperturbable beauty.
Wisps of breath embroider our speech,
cartoon bubbles that hang in the air then melt
into the slush, into some deep significance
we're not responsible for.

Lighthouse

We do not need to be shown the sea
the way those in ships need to see the shore,
need to know what could ruin a landfall.
On a clear winter's day this beacon, housing
only ghosts, illuminates us regardless, the
understanding we've reached.
We stare down the long drop to the sea,
watch multicoloured dreams of flight

supported by the wind. Practised now
at averting disaster, we have jettisoned
some baggage. Under a stark unfiltered sky
the tin-foil brilliance of the waves lights up,
like a camera's flash, what it's taken us
years to discern.

Transparency

I pass slide after slide from left to right,
keeping fingers clear of the image – a cache
neglected for years. I'm feeding them into
an Agfa viewer like flat tropical fish –
predictably amazing, predictably opaque –
thin slices of history, now history themselves.
It seems at times *transparencies* could
have been better named.

The viewer illuminates colour and shape,
but narrative hides in the shadows –
you could read more in a stained-glass window
on a heritage afternoon.
Faces, backlit by a feeble bulb, seem to accuse
my eye: is *this* all you remember?

Last slide in the box, and a long grey bridge
drops out of a cloudless sky.
I keep holding it up to the light, but nothing
will spill out – not sadness, not even guilt,
just your face as you stand beside me
while I juggle the perfect shot.

Five-finger Exercise

This morning at breakfast, peeling an orange
pretty much in silence – why, for instance,
not then?
Why now, with a book to distract you,
lying at the edge of a pool within earshot of
the beach –
one idle hand trailing in water as if that
were its natural home; the squeals of children
and the ocean's percussion filtered out
with the u/v.

And then, between the distant waves,
you hear an unmistakeable voice declaring,
apropos of nothing: *you know, you've got
beautiful hands* –
words that turn up like overlooked coins
announcing themselves in the dryer, her voice
slipping under your guard like a splinter
under a nail.
Then the tears that surprise you, but
shouldn't, not even at this remove.

And you really don't care if anyone's looking
as you hold up your freshwater catch – dappled
pink, still dripping chlorine – and, if she insists,
beautiful, as are most hands.

Piano

Something about returning. Something
about this room – a figure purporting to be you
appears, if I close my eyes.
How the silence gathers you in, amplifies
your absence. I admit you into this space, but
discern no change in the light except for
the passage of clouds.
You appear little the worse for wear, for
the year-long lack of sunlight.

I allow my mind to wander, and the keys
depress and release by themselves as if on
a pianola – a row of creamy and pot-black teeth
chewing on something inside. I imagine a
small brown dog on the rug, untroubled
by the sound.

Sooner or later my fingers return to the
scales we used to practise. Your fingers
join in, confident, in sync, grateful
for company.

Johannes & Clara

Brahms died the year after Clara, useless,
it seems, without her.
Not that he ever was, entirely –
the older woman filled his heart the way
a note can fill a piano, the way air
fills what we call the sky. It can feel
like overflowing.

In their singular beds they lay
straight up & down, their pillows never
touching.
More than one way to skin a heart –
soulmates, people can tell. Someone
to live, or not live for.

They remained well-matched to the end,
death certificates notwithstanding:
Clara dies of a bleeding brain, Brahms
of a washed-out heart.

The Night Shift

Coming to bed as I used to, back then,
in the cold trough of the night, it was my hands
that would announce me, their warmth lost
between bathroom tap and the site
of your regular breathing.
You'd flinch as your barely conscious skin,
discerning as that of a waking body, registered
my touch –
shrinking from me as you'd once fled
the schoolboys with ice cubes tucked in
their hands.

You'd recoil from my hands as if they
were meat for your vegan flesh to avoid, or
the icy flippers of a penguin conjured,
mysteriously, into our bed – as if,
in the dark, they might quietly unfold
into the cold wings of death.

All in the Mind

1 Blueberries

We are binary as computers, our hemispheres
tend that way. Yet the right and left sides of
the brain won't stop talking to each other –
a dialogue not fully decoded.
Traditional labels grow heavy in our hands,
waiting for us to attach them: *Unstable. Requires
medication.* Who is to say when you'll next
take off, radiant with Truth?

You've been up & down the street since daybreak,
arms outstretched, chanting, beaming away
the stares of joggers and people out
walking their dogs.
Now you're sitting up next to me in bed,
still slightly out of breath, with a small bowl of
blueberries icy from the fridge. Each berry
resisting the warmth of my mouth, like
you resisting cold reason.

2 Dirt on the Tongue

You're out in the yard not long after sunrise,
stuffing your mouth full of earth.
Under a doona, in the grip of a dream, I am
unaware of your absence.
Eventually you climb back into bed, tell me
about the soil and its taste, how you've been
trying to remove it with a cake of
laundry soap –
sane enough, suddenly, to wryly admit
that the cure can indeed be worse;
to assure me you're perfectly fine again
and yes, I can go off to work.

Kids I knew had mothers who threatened
to wash their mouth out with soap;
not schooled in the zealot's vocabulary –
mortification, atonement – I thought
it was some kind of joke.
Guilt and delusion have the best antennae,
hear signals you wouldn't believe – pick up
voices from anywhere, turn whispers
into a roar.

Photo Negative

We died in a roll of unprocessed film,
our story curled up like a scroll, or dry leaf –
locked into a shiny black cylinder like the
dead in a submarine.
Twelve months in suspended animation,
we were ebbing slowly, dot by dot, as the
emulsion raced towards expiry –
two fading photochemical ghosts misplaced
at the back of my office drawer by some
half-accidental design, or by someone
divining the future.

It hardly mattered, with only one witness
to flesh out the images – one strip
of celluloid history that wouldn't survive
to haunt me.
The roll hit the floor of the wheelie bin
like a car hitting a wall –
the sound died abruptly, while upstairs,
inside a photo album, you were laughing
to raise the dead.

What Can't Be Held

Some time before dawn I become aware
I am sharing the bed with your selves –
versions of you that compete for attention,
winning out over sleep –

like you stepping out of the shower, shoulders
beaded with clusters of drops, unfamiliar for
a moment under a mask of wet hair;
like the small muscles at work on your back
as you start drying yourself, stopping to notice
a love bite;
like you half asleep, or totally present, all
the times your voice seemed the essence of you,
and laughter the essence of voice –

selves that never add up to the whole,
glimpses of an installation designed not to
stop changing – images melting, recombining,
drifting back out of focus; yet an installation
not abstract enough to give up its grip
on the heart.

Rock Face With Wattle

You were all feeling, and consequently
that much less use to the world.
Though you did well enough, god knows –
survived the older sister, played tennis for your
school, then kept a bevy of lawyers afloat
above their oceans of paper.
Survived the treatments that jolted your body
while purporting to heal your mind.

We lived, for a time, at the top of a cutting
that sprouted wild clusters of wattle, looked down
on a road that fed car after car into the mouth
of the city.
Steel mesh covered the rock like a hairnet
to save the traffic from scree; nothing, however,
could stop golden wattle dislodging its
heavy scent.

Scientists who may have trapped insects as
children are now trapping light in a jar, determined
to ward off the dark – glimmers from the edge
of some galaxy even God has wiped from
the tape.
And I can't erase a single thing, not you
crying in my arms on a bed in a country hotel –
too close to the pain you had never forgotten,
too distant, you felt, from me.

Half-life

The current that flows through your radio
lives on, though it died at the wall – switch it
back on absentmindedly, and a zombie voice
sparks into life for a disconcerting instant.
You glance warily in its direction, like a guard
checking the death chamber walls for a
crack the spirit might slip through –
understanding the physics of death well enough,
yet afraid that the guy has his number.

In underground cables, anonymous spaces,
life proceeds out of sight – the low-voltage hum
of unfinished business awaiting resolution.
In this city, briefly, for work, you turn a corner
and run into your past: meeting her eyes – first
time in how long – shocked, yet unsurprised;
as if you had never stopped waiting for
this small hard fist to your gut.

You'd expected reproach, but not a face
so flooded with dismay; your self-imposed
sentence extended now to something
like life and a day.

Repair Job

Surgeons mended it, and, of course, the
body's own superglue – if the mind has a mind
to live. She fractured it, that heart of yours,
never put to the test by your wife –
you with a heart-shaped target pinned
to the hologram of your life.

I suspect you didn't entirely regret it:
hooking up, after so many years, with
someone you'd lusted after.
Who went on to say you were great in bed,
but what else could she use you for?
More or less showed you the door.

Recovered, back to your old self, and changed,
your long-ago wife in a different country, you
took from it what you had to.
I believe your heart grew stronger each year,
so much time still up your sleeve –
hearty in the land of the living, finished
with make-believe.

Inscription

I'm holding his book in my hand – a brilliant
poet who drank too much, and never pulled his
punches.
It's years since I last took him on, years since
you & I consented to each other's hands.

A poet with a wicked hook who's caught me
off-guard again – my stomach working hard to
recover some of my buckled breath.
Once I'd have blamed my poor defences
on the words inside the cover – so pointed
with happiness the day you wrote them, they
overwhelmed the book; words that have
punched the air for so long now they
merely deliver nostalgia.

Old combatants growing slow on our feet,
our shadow-boxing today would most likely
damage only ourselves.
The poet you chose so unerringly then
is still alive & kicking, lethal as a Thai boxer –
a contestant with total surprise on his side,
like the chute that fails to open.

On the Eve

An ill-fitting comparison, granted.
All the same, I'm reminded of the soldier
who, having heard *We advance tomorrow,*
assumes he's already dead –
who eats his rations, and in the morning
rolls up his bed with the crisp contempt
the dead reserve for the living.

I inhale the stillness as if it were peace,
imagine this space closing behind you like
water over one's head –
you, more than halfway gone already, you
who've been absent too long;
you who continue criss-crossing the floor
as if to throw off pursuit.
You, whose slow breathing is readily traced
down the hall and into our room –

sounds that could take their place alongside
human testaments launched into space –
hopeful ambassadors for the species,
the longest of our long shots –
which day by day leave us further behind,
no matter where they'll end up.

Jackknifed

Still think of you as sweet, your intentions
not at all evil. Hadn't seen the train wreck coming –
jackknifed my heart, couldn't speak.
A silence more than long enough for you
to slip away –
kind of a virtual absence, your outline
persisting day after day as if you'd been
sculpted in Braille.

Must admit the guy you left me for had a
more commercial body – could have done
part-time modelling, wearing his glasses,
or not; as it was, he was teaching group
meditation, with massage on the side.
Married a French girl not long after –
Hong Kong, as I recall – remembered
to send you photos.

You had friends to pick up the pieces;
he had her, and his other calling.
The lessons you both taught me, basic
as crossing a road –
once recklessly ready to jump, now
more than wary of falling.

Bandage

I'll peel off the imprint of your skin – a
kind of film clinging for weeks like a dressing
ignored too long.

Healed or not, a wound needs to breathe
some ordinary air, receive its quota of sunlight,
retrieve its feel for the world.
The exposed tissue is either unsightly
or may remind you of opal, if your aesthetics
permits – either way, distinctly less morbid than
the fluorescent, mortuary blue of cells cut off
from circulation.

It's late. I'll peel you off in the morning –
one swift, decisive gesture, a sharp twinge,
and it's over at last.
The heart, not as wounded and missing you
less, I'll still carry a while in a sling.
Confidence is what is called for – let's see
what a new skin can bring.

A Voyeur Welcomes September

Well-dressed, he looks his profession, with a
pale baggy face and a middle-aged heart he'd
contend is devoid of malice.
Spends lunchtimes in a park near the office,
a broadsheet for protection – can't resist the
flash of earrings and bangles, the lipstick-
shiny voices.

His eyes, discreet as he can make them,
circle the breasts that seem out of sync with
faces still grounded in childhood.
The youngsters skate around him, laughing,
he's part and not part of their game; confident
in their performance, they don't stop to look
his way. He sucks in his breath, as sincere in
his feeling as an early line by Wordsworth.

Every spring their handed-down beauty
catches him unprepared; one more noiseless
click of a dial that will never stop turning.
In the wilderness of a leafy suburb, home is
a wife who doesn't make trouble, a wife
who perhaps understands;
home is a place to play, late at night, with
the gap between virtual and real, a mouse
in his velvet hand.

Player

He's been following her for years – a loser
who knows when he's winning, a stalker
who's paid at the gate.
He enjoys watching her sweat, could run
through the sequence, if asked.
She sweats from the backbone outwards –
a dark line at the start, then muscle and bone
collude to form a trough that will steadily
widen.

She works the ball, the dampness spreads,
her back assumes a life of its own –
she grunts, cries out, as if in the business of
simulating sex; begins to bad-mouth an umpire
who is good at reading lips, turns linesmen
to stone with her eyes.
She attacks every ball, a love/hate object
to be pounded into submission. What else
to live for right now?
In the stalls, indifferent to the outcome,
he's untouchable as Buddha.

On-court fashion is everyone's friend, as much
on his side as on hers –
her legs are great, but too obvious, she can
choose what people will see.
And *he* loves conspiracy – the way sweat
sells off her privacy, behind her back,
for free.

The Tan

She disappears beneath her sunscreen,
slips away on its oily fragrance, her passport
to out of here –
here where she knows pretty much what's
expected, here where the body has to contend
with someone else's head. Which right now
is at the Casino.

She's parked herself on a long pink towel,
like a commuter leaving their car on the frayed
edge of the city.
While the sun goes about its work, she feels
her fists unclenching;
working her way back into her head, she
lets random thoughts ascend like kites above
the cries of the gulls.
While she is absent beads of sweat
collect between her breasts – pearls mixed
with the odd grain of sand.

In their hotel room she'll check herself out,
satisfied enough, and the mirror will wink
& nudge. She's got her role down pat,
has prepared a brown goddess for him.
Doesn't know about his plans.

Plum-coloured Days

The New Year comes out of its corner fighting,
beer on its breath, side-stepping the ref, lashing out
at the heat and the boredom and the deadly lack
of prospects – rage is a contact sport, can't
get by just punching air.
Words of remorse, acts of atonement, chase
each disaster like a tow truck but don't reach the
scene in time. While he's out she'll phone a
friend, most likely ignore their advice.

Mulberry stains spread under her eyes, plums
ripen on her arms, marks so vivid it's hard to
believe they'll fade like they always have –
unlike the tat she has grown to hate, or that
nickname she can't shake.
Skin and heart are indifferent pupils, there
are lessons that just won't take.

The Business

He'll be gone by the time the client arrives –
a few hours' worth of Bloom-like absence –
taking his alibi down to the shops, steering
a trolley down the aisles while the wife
is turning a trick – bringing home the
bacon, taking in some prick.

He'll stop for a drink or two while he's out,
a beer or two with her blessing, free for
a special few.
His back to the chain gang noise of the pokies
he'll watch the guys & girls playing pool,
their butts encased in soft denim – how they
fetish-fondle the cues, practising cat & mouse.
Playing the games you need to play before
you start playing house.

Back home, he'll find her the same,
or in any event, close enough. They're legal,
or near enough – business partners with
benefits, turning clichés into cash:
Whatever It Takes. Just Do It. *Battlers*
sounds too much like *trash*.

Hotel

She pulls back her hair, secures it. Her neck,
still hot, bends over a lighter.
Five minutes to catch her breath. She
inhales something like freedom, freshens
her mouth with nicotine, blows smoke
at the bathroom wall.

Her face is not like your four-star website,
more of an all-purpose mask –
some detect a residual innocence, some
imagine her with pearls; she plays out remote
as a video clip, makes up soundtracks
to suit the mood.
In my Father's house are many rooms,
and each has a hotel bed –
Babylon to Kings Cross, she is fish scales
or golden serpent, it depends on the
state of your head.
No one is hurt and no one forgiven,
in the end it's a driverless car.

She crosses the lobby, free for an hour,
her legs no clue to her age.
Reception follows her out with his eyes
then goes back to swiping a screen.

Pleasure & Pain

If human history is a guide, there are more
ways of inflicting pain than of delivering
pleasure.
As far as we can measure, this applies
to both psyche and skin – though the soul,
unlike endangered reefs, tries to mask
the damage within.
There are psyches clogged from an early age
with old religion's silt – some keep whipping
the same bloodied self in the name of
some nameless guilt.

A fine line between pleasure and pain,
The Divynils said it so well. There are those
who trade pain for the pleasure it gives them,
at whatever rate of exchange; yet trying to
meet pain's interest bills is a tough way
of paying your dues. Pleasure & pain
draw up their own contract, the fine print
is seldom good news.

Another Country

If I were to grow breasts and start bleeding,
I could sell my story for cash.
Even less likely is finding a way to observe,
from within, a human machine translating the
words I speak.
Each person's mind is a foreign grammar,
a syntax we can't quite decode; a logic
too private to fathom, an uncharted
mother-lode.

Believing ourselves misunderstood, we
rely more and more on stance – though few
can match the humpback whale who's learned
how to balance on his head while singing
to his mate.
Perhaps water's a happier medium than
what we've been floundering in.

On land, the air hums with transmissions –
signals drop in & out, sunspots unleash
their own static.
If we don't find a way to cut through,
we'll turn into algorithms, our responses
automatic.

This Love

It's not a lot of use to us – this pit-bull love
bred to hang on, clamping its jaws regardless;
a love that, ignoring the sentence, has
thrown away the key.

A love that likes to play Captain, though it
can't control the vessel, has never outsailed
a storm; that keeps wishing us a good trip,
though it sold off the lifeboats years ago
when it had a gambling problem. That says
we can't jump ship.

This love's a magician who has lost faith in
the power of illusion; this love is a suit we keep
trying on, though it's never fitted us yet;
this love will corner us at a party and ask
what it is we regret.

This love may be howling at the moon but
we no longer hear it. This love has managed
to blur the line between a greyhound and
rabbit; this love's not religion, just opium,
and we can't kick the habit.

Saving the Day

A thorn in my side, a stone in your shoe –
we irritate each other. Isn't that our true function,
isn't that how pearls are made? Ok, let's
drop the folk wisdom –
there must be more creative ways to keep
the juices flowing, to generate a voltage
that doesn't put paid to the heart.

A provocation, an ill-judged word: how
easy to disrupt a day and see it fall apart –
instantly back in each other's face, a move
we've practised so well; adrenalin-fuelled
in our corners, poised for the sound of
the bell.

Facing off, we forget what we know, are
not in the mood for new learning;
unable to save the day, we're forced
to watch the night burning.

Saving the Night

Remember Scheherazade, the palace
her gilded cage – Shahryar's next victim,
her life on the line, hoping each night for
reprieve. Living one day at a time,
jealous women's ankle bells following
her like whispers.

Fabulous Scheherazade, working to save
her life with her mouth, that is to say, with her
quicksilver mind and database of stories,
and a tongue to give voice to invention.
Not that stories alone were enough –
in between holding her breath, she lived
death after little death.

Can't say she didn't communicate, can't
say it didn't pay off. So, what is holding us
back?
Skin can light fires on skin, passion's
sure-fire revival; but then there's the kindling
of words, the other great tool of survival.

Crowded

Three's a crowd, but that's how we sleep,
or four to a bed, at times – just life, not a
swingers' party. The singularity of two
exists mosty in dreams.

Summoned or not, ex lovers appear, visible
only to us; obliging our need for approval,
our wish to avoid their disdain.
Control freaks still, if that's what they were,
they may hold up a veto sign, attempting
to sway their host – messengers we
can't shoot, bullet-proof as ghosts.

Happy to leave us in doubt, old lovers
tend to slip away once they have taken stock.
New lovers – like the one with me tonight –
are liable to shock: she calls me
by a stranger's name, so intent, I let her
use it –
I won't get to thank him for the loan,
but all the same don't refuse it.

Old Flame

You patrol the horizon of our world
as strictly as a coastguard, taking care
to keep him to bay – a phantom submarine
out to sea, too distant to be spotted
even at your heart's low tide.

In the dark we don't mention his name –
if he ever surfaces for you, he's not there
to test my eyesight, tied as it is
to good lighting; sun-averse as your
average ghost, he makes sure
he is gone by morning.

You manage to clear him from your face
like swiping a laptop screen;
like ridding yourself of a secret vice
before it is even suspected. Like
someone performing a generous act
that may never be detected.

The Debt

Who's to be trusted, after he's gone,
to be stopping her mouth with his hand –
should silence be required –
at least long enough for a scar to form,
for memories to be filed?

For he'd barely trusted himself at times,
bent over her, half present, happily serving
the cause.
A choice, he hopes, she will make with
due care, despite the temptation to rush –
a task as tricky as that of a crime boss
naming a successor, or a magistrate
modelling truth.

It's just that he feels he owes her.
For her unspectacular loyalty, for each
time he felt, in the moment, that he owed
some stranger more –
their leather jacket, their talent, that
adrenalin knock on the door.

The Desire Between Them

The desire between them is always there,
no matter how others translate it –
the perennial elephant in the room
acknowledged in silences, or turned into
a bargaining chip; in the no-man's land
between loving and strife, it does
the best it can.
If it could, it would start each day afresh,
its elephant slate wiped clean;
but slights live on in a memory bank that
surrenders no more than it has to.

The desire between them, should
it desert them, would be material loss –
beyond the broken mirror's bad luck,
beyond a stolen passport.
It would not matter in the end if it fell
to outside forces, was indecisive for years,
or left overnight without packing.

Whale Song

Guess we never made successful whales,
humping to a standstill, undertaking migrations,
lost in the mindless blue.
Don't get me wrong, I know whales have
minds, and very fine ones, at that. But
you get my drift.
We were more like goldfish, I guess –
ears tucked out of sight, enjoying the gaze
of the curious, amusing them without trying;
or sometimes, feeling wicked, pulling
seaweed over their eyes.

Seems the relationship was the leviathan
shadowing us all along, swallowing us as we
slept – two Jonahs for the price of one;
and when we emerged at last, it was surely
none the wiser.
Fabulous is the whale at sea, balancing
excess and style, resisting the lure of the
beach; a navigational skill we found
forever out of reach.

Charcoal

An interstate bus in the rain.
Windscreen wipers arguing, incessantly,
with rain – robotic arms that have us believing
they are dictating our motion, the driver
a marionette, hypnotised like us.
Our vision reduced to this: two hemispheres
cleared for a moment or two, some of us
viewing the world through lenses that
won't stop fogging up.
Hungry for colour, we'd kill for a movie
but the only movie is this –

a low grey ceiling of a sky, dripping into
a carpet of grass more or less the colour of
Ireland; the whole world looks the same
in the rain.
And a long, unwavering highway that is
really no colour at all, but fades in & out of
charcoal, dividing green from green.
By tonight it will seem like a week,
too long to be lost for words; fading in &
out of the night before, we search for
the will to begin.

Phoney War

Weeks of blue skies, unimpeded horizons,
crisp days you could stack like firewood, like
grievances biding their time. Or not, as
we are finding. The rain, when it comes,
is a brief distraction, recolonising our heads
like a language we thought we'd forgotten.
But thunder, this far into autumn? –
weird as unexplained lights in the sky
or a camel loose in Kings Cross.

Safe on the deck we watch lightning strikes,
impressed in the way of small children.
How a storm commandeers the atmosphere,
switching our voltage around, polarising
moods; the luxury of surrendering to its
brief, predictable violence. There's
a real war happening on TV, but we've
chosen a softer option.

Little Red Devil

Here you are, the two of you, in the ring again,
trying to fight clean.
Or, if you will, centre stage again, reciting
familiar lines.

When *this* guy lands, it's not in a spotlight,
nor in a blaze of trumpets –
this is no deity intervening while mortals
hurriedly shield their eyes and defer to the
wisdom of gods.
In your war of words this weird little guy
is no Netflix hero for justice, no advocate
for your cause –
just a dodgy double agent, concealing
a fine-print clause.

At each turn of your stand-off a little red
devil sneaks up behind the pair you, whispers
in both sets of ears, poisons both sets
of arrows. You fall down, on cue, every
time. I guess it's the perfect crime.

Street Theatre

Passing us on the street, people observe
only unity, like crows flying in pairs –
a surface show of harmony, *and* without
the discordant cries; birds of a certain feather,
inclined to disagree.
Is it temperament, breeding, conviction,
this mutual wish to spare outsiders the private
face of strife – the reflex, defensive snarl of
gargoyles frozen in soot-covered stone;
the inborn flair for the drama you can't
practise on your own.

Players conscripted into this theatre flail about
like puppets at the whim of invisible hands –
confused, except for the rage, like a bull
set up for the kill; naively, touchingly
brave, all too publicly alone.
We've agreed not to play Punch & Judy,
to save our quarrels for home.

Title Fight

You're sleeping, but the contest between us
keeps humming like the long black nerves
strung from pylon to pylon – a subliminal
heavy metal bass that resonates with
the earth.
We've declared a ceasefire, if only because
we've run out of ammunition –
a fragile peace, now & then broken
by possums thudding onto the deck like
outsize overripe mangoes.
Even so, you barely stir in your sleep;
truce hovers above our bed.

I pace a makeshift boxing ring,
feeling unexpectedly free despite such close
confinement. Besides, in the dark, I could
slip through the ropes anytime I wanted.
In a moment or two I will join you –
ahead on points, I believe, but uneasy,
rehearsing tomorrow's strategy, doubling
as personal coach.

Breathing deeply next to each other,
towing self-contained trailers of dreams
that collide despite ourselves, we won't
be aware of white-coated figures, noiseless
on rubber soles, monitoring our heart rate,
clearing us for another round, placing
bets on the outcome –
eager for a clear result, or resigned to
more of the same.

And in the morning, no debris,
no shards from a plate someone had thrown,
just a fresh southerly breeze.
We make our way down to the car
without speaking, notice how possums
have torn fresh strips off their current
tree of choice – tongues of dry bark
fluttering, half attached, half free.

Truce

Not nearly as deadly as combat: I'm not
the soldier of legend – or fact – the pocket
bible in his coat his only bullet-proof vest;
his faith compressed into that space,
survival his holy proof.
But then, your words are hardly bullets,
though aimed equally at the head –
which, no less vulnerable than the heart,
is easily pressed into service, a willing
servant of feeling.

It's for head and heart to listen out, the
tongue to offer terms of peace the moment
a white flag is raised.
A human skin, if carefully peeled and
somehow stitched together, might offer a
tabula rasa, whatever the colour of choice.
Stitch up my head with your words, let's
reclaim our peacetime voice.

You Never Saw Yourself

You never saw yourself asleep – so far as
you let on. You'd read accounts of near-death
events, the consciousness floating free –
it intrigued you, a spirit observing its body
from just below the ceiling, or circling its home
like a hawk.
Never got, all the same, to see your sleeping
form through another's eyes –
invincible without your defences, drained
of all fear and hostility, forgiven
there & then.

Never saw yourself removed from the world,
untouched, untouchable – totally out of the loop,
basic as an infant – an equation so
readily solved, all my matching hostilities
would evaporate on the spot.
Only to form again, the next day, the
fine human rain of mistrust.

All Quiet at the End of the Street

When the latest showdown has run out of steam,
when logic has run out of sense –
most parties tend to shut their mouth, close
a window they'd overlooked.

From the heart of contested territory,
the blurt of another confessional broadcast
to those still awake – as if, exposed
in the darkness of bedrooms, we needed
lessons in strife.
By & by the street gets itself off to sleep,
having half expected to hear someone's voice
rising from the ashes. Which, in the end,
it may not – only so long you can make your
case before you're too tired to care.

Working our way towards justice, we speak
in the tongue of self-justification –
if our disembodied voices had shape,
they might resemble two bare-arsed koalas
glued to their tree by a spotlight, unaware
of their starring role in a midnight
suburban shoot.
How dry in the mouth we get, working
our way towards silence.

Cooling Down

We've been fighting, you've been beating
your fists against my intractable wall –
your version, slanted as mine.
It's taken us years to give up on logic, to
realise neither will bleed to death skewered
on a word. It's exhausting, even so, and
you opt for an early night.

You won't be aware of this rain, its muffled,
fluctuating heartbeat borrowing from ours;
won't notice the frantic flickering of a
streetlight refusing to die.
Cool air starts to settle on our skin,
your sleepwalking hand plucks at the sheet
I pull up over your shoulder, my fingers
blending seamlessly with those in
your virtual world.

Outside, a massive eucalypt trunk glistens
like a fat man in a sauna, its pink hide sweating
a pearly fever that may be gone by morning.
Sleep can be our referee, holding up a
score card tomorrow if we still want
to know.

Midnight Radio

A radio shields you from the dark, a film
of sound that protects you like lead from the
night's cool radiation.
Invisible waves break on your body,
supplanting the bedside lamp; low decibels
that merge with your breathing without
alarming your mind –
a movie theme, news of trouble in China,
stock market figures at close of trade
share the space around your head, drift
over you like clouds.

You are distilling the day. Your arteries brim
with theorems, your veins carry messages
miraculously in sync –
a quantum world designed to keep chaos
out of the everyday.
You appear perfectly whole; a challenge for
the waking. You've reverted to pure possibility,
seem open to starting afresh. Could I ever
feel closer, ever know you less?

A Night Off For the Moon

Tonight the moon can be just the moon,
I'll try to stop it gatecrashing the poem that's
been following me around.
Under a vapour trail of stars I'll set off
on my nightly voyage – a landlubber sailing
by the unfailing beacons of TV towers,
red warning lights glowing like cigarettes
in mouths that can only inhale.

I may pass sites of magical thinking where
people still trust the universe to indulge
their smoking in bed.
Like three wise monkeys rolled into one
I'll stroll undeterred past haunted houses,
wondering what secrets we share.
I'll follow the veins of badly lit streets
that lead to the same anonymous heart
to make mine beat a little faster.

My feet on auto pilot, I'll recall, without trying,
things I'd forgotten, while rehearsing
what everyone knows.
Out in deep space time loses the plot, but
down here we know which way it flows.

Acknowledgements

I would like to thank the editors of the following publications in which a number of these poems first appeared, mostly in earlier versions:

The Age; Agenda (UK); *The Weekend Australian Review*; *The Best Australian Poems 2006* (ed. Dorothy Porter); *The Best Australian Poems 2011* (ed. John Tranter); *The Canberra Times; Eureka Street; Imago*; Interactive Press 20th anniversary anthology 2017; *Island*; Melbourne Poetry Festival anthology 1999; Newcastle Poetry Prize anthology 1995; *Outrider; Papertiger; Stylus; Voices* (National Library of Australia).

I would like also to acknowledge Arts Queensland, the sState government's arts funding body, for support in completing the first draft of this collection.

'Geological Time' first appeared, in an earlier version, in *Facing the Pacific*, Interactive Press 1999

www.ingramcontent.com/pod-product-compliance
Lightning Source LLC
Chambersburg PA
CBHW071009080526
44587CB00015B/2406